It's a Beautiful Day!

of the Tiny Seekers Series

for all the tiny kings and queens of this universe
Aida, especially you

Emily June Ellis

This book belongs to the Tiny Seeker,

____

Little Seeker,

Wake up!
Do you feel the
LOVE
all around?

Magic awaits our day ahead!

Listen closely
to
Mother Nature's
sounds!

The morning dew glistens
to the birds and bees sweet song.

If you tune in
MINDFULLY,
you can sing along!

The sun is smiling
and shining light on us
ALL,

No matter the creatures,
BIG
and
small!

Let's brush our teeth
with the
rhythm around,

Dress and
HURRY
to the endless
adventures abound!

Barefoot
in the grass
is
ALWAYS
best,

But today is calling for
socks and shoes,
cause there's no time for rest!

Be sure to fill your belly with
wholesome bread,
veggies, and fruit,

For it's time to
EXPLORE
the world!

Come on!
Let's scoot!

First,
take a
DEEP
breath
as you go outdoors,

Feel the cool breeze,
open all your
SENSES,
and you'll see much more!

Now,
before
you
run and play,

Remember
to live in the present
and be SO very
grateful about
this
BEAUTIFUL
DAY!

There's no telling
what you'll find,

When you
OPEN
your
HEART
and
FREE
your
LIMITLESS
mind!

Brave child
of this universe,
JOURNEY
wild and wide!

Absolutely nothing can stop you!
&
Get EXCITED!
Just wait to see what you will do!

IT'S FOREVER TRUE!

It sure is a beautiful day.

The End.

www.ingramcontent.com/pod-product-compliance
Lightning Source LLC
Chambersburg PA
CBHW081300090726
47818CB00079B/202